C000260478

Francis Frith's

Yorkshire
Living Memories

Francis Frith's
Yorkshire Living Memories

Roly Smith

First published in hardback in the United Kingdom in 2000 by
The Francis Frith Collection®
ISBN 1-85937-166-3

Paperback edition 2001
ISBN 1-85937-397-6
Reprinted in paperback 2005

Text and Design copyright The Francis Frith Collection®
Photographs copyright The Francis Frith Collection®
except where indicated.

The Frith® photographs and the Frith® logo are reproduced under licence from
Heritage Photographic Resources Ltd, the owners of the Frith® archive and trademarks.
'The Francis Frith Collection', 'Francis Frith' and 'Frith' are registered trademarks of
Heritage Photographic Resources Ltd.

All rights reserved. No photograph in this publication may be sold to a third party other than in the original
form of this publication, or framed for sale to a third party. No parts of this publication may be reproduced,
stored in a retrieval system, or transmitted, in any form, or by any means, electronic,
mechanical, photocopying, recording or otherwise, without the prior permission of the
publishers and copyright holder.

British Library Cataloguing in Publication Data

Yorkshire Living Memories
Roly Smith
ISBN 1-85937-397-6

The Francis Frith Collection
Frith's Barn, Teffont,
Salisbury, Wiltshire SP3 5QP
Tel: +44 (0) 1722 716 376
Email: info@francisfrith.co.uk
www.francisfrith.co.uk

Printed and bound in Great Britain

Front Cover: Skipton, High Street c1955 S137035t

The colour-tinting is for illustrative purposes only, and is not intended to be historically accurate

Every attempt has been made to contact copyright holders of illustrative material.
We will be happy to give full acknowledgement in future editions for any items not credited.
Any information should be directed to The Francis Frith Collection.

As with any historical database the Frith archive is constantly being corrected and improved
and the publishers would welcome information on omissions or inaccuracies

Contents

Francis Frith: *Victorian Pioneer*

FRANCIS FRITH, Victorian founder of the world-famous photographic archive, was a complex and multitudinous man. A devout Quaker and a highly successful Victorian businessman, he was both philosophical by nature and pioneering in outlook.

By 1855 Francis Frith had already established a wholesale grocery business in Liverpool, and sold it for the astonishing sum of £200,000, which is the equivalent today of over £15,000,000. Now a very rich man, he was able to indulge his passion for travel. As a child he had pored over travel books written by early explorers, and his fancy and imagination had been stirred by family holidays to the sublime mountain regions of Wales and Scotland. 'What lands of spirit-stirring and enriching scenes and places!' he had written. He was to return to these scenes of grandeur in later years to 'recapture the thousands of vivid and tender memories', but with a different purpose. Now in his thirties, and captivated by the new science of photography, Frith set out on a series of pioneering journeys to the Nile regions that occupied him from 1856 until 1860.

Intrigue and Adventure

He took with him on his travels a specially-designed wicker carriage that acted as both dark-room and sleeping chamber. These far-flung journeys were packed with intrigue and adventure. In his life story, written when he was sixty-three, Frith tells of being held captive by bandits, and of fighting 'an awful midnight battle to the very point of surrender with a deadly pack of hungry, wild dogs'. Sporting flowing Arab costume, Frith arrived at Akaba by camel sixty years before Lawrence, where he encountered 'desert princes and rival sheikhs, blazing with jewel-hilted swords'.

During these extraordinary adventures he was assiduously exploring the desert regions bordering the Nile and patiently recording the antiquities and peoples with his camera. He was the first photographer to venture beyond the sixth cataract. Africa was still the mysterious 'Dark Continent', and Stanley and Livingstone's historic meeting was a decade into the future. The conditions for picture taking confound belief. He laboured for hours in his wicker dark-room in the sweltering heat of the desert, while the volatile chemicals fizzed dangerously in their trays. Often he was forced to work in remote tombs and caves where conditions were cooler. Back in London he exhibited his photographs and was 'rapturously cheered' by members of the Royal Society. His reputation as a photographer was made overnight. An eminent modern historian has likened their impact on the population of the time to that on our own generation of the first photographs taken on the surface of the moon.

Venture of a Life-Time

Characteristically, Frith quickly spotted the opportunity to create a new business as a specialist publisher of photographs. He lived in an era of immense and sometimes violent change. For the poor in the early part of Victoria's reign work was a drudge and the hours long, and people had precious little free time to enjoy themselves. Most had no transport other than a cart or gig at their disposal, and had not travelled far beyond the boundaries of their own town or village. However, by the 1870s, the railways had threaded their way across the country, and Bank Holidays and half-day Saturdays had been made obligatory by Act of Parliament. All of a sudden the ordinary working man and his family were able to enjoy days out and see a little more of the world.

With characteristic business acumen, Francis Frith foresaw that these new tourists would enjoy having souvenirs to commemorate their days out. In 1860 he married Mary Ann Rosling and set out with the intention of photographing every city, town and village in Britain. For the next thirty years he travelled the country by train and by pony and trap, producing fine photographs of seaside resorts and beauty spots that were keenly bought by millions of Victorians. These prints were painstakingly pasted into family albums and pored over during the dark nights of winter, rekindling precious memories of summer excursions.

The Rise of Frith & Co

Frith's studio was soon supplying retail shops all over the country. To meet the demand he gathered about him a small team of photographers, and published the work of independent artist-photographers of the calibre of Roger Fenton and Francis Bedford. In order to gain some understanding of the scale of Frith's business one only has to look at the catalogue issued by Frith & Co in 1886: it runs to some 670 pages, listing not only many thousands of views of the British Isles but also many photographs of most European countries, and China, Japan, the USA and Canada – note the sample page shown on page 9 from the hand-written *Frith & Co* ledgers

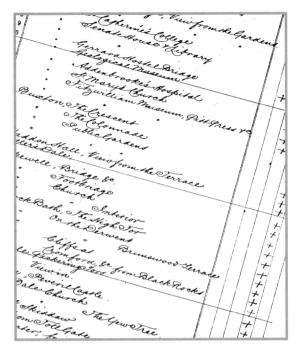

detailing pictures taken. By 1890 Frith had created the greatest specialist photographic publishing company in the world, with over 2,000 outlets – more than the combined number that Boots and W H Smith have today! The picture on the right shows the *Frith & Co* display board at Ingleton in the Yorkshire Dales (left of window). Beautifully constructed with a mahogany frame and gilt inserts, it could display up to a dozen local scenes.

Postcard Bonanza

The ever-popular holiday postcard we know today took many years to develop. In 1870 the Post Office issued the first plain cards, with a pre-printed stamp on one face. In 1894 they allowed other publishers' cards to be sent through the mail with an attached adhesive halfpenny stamp. Demand grew rapidly, and in 1895 a new size of postcard was permitted called the court card, but there was little room for

illustration. In 1899, a year after Frith's death, a new card measuring 5.5 x 3.5 inches became the standard format, but it was not until 1902 that the divided back came into being, with address and message on one face and a full-size illustration on the other. *Frith & Co* were in the vanguard of postcard development, and Frith's sons Eustace and Cyril continued their father's monumental task, expanding the number of views offered to the public and recording more and more places in Britain, as the coasts and countryside were opened up to mass travel.

Francis Frith died in 1898 at his villa in Cannes, his great project still growing. The archive he created continued in business for another seventy years. By 1970 it contained over a third of a million pictures of 7,000 cities, towns and villages. The massive photographic record Frith has left to us stands as a living monument to a special and very remarkable man.

Frith's Archive: *A Unique Legacy*

FRANCIS FRITH'S legacy to us today is of immense significance and value, for the magnificent archive of evocative photographs he created provides a unique record of change in 7,000 cities, towns and villages throughout Britain over a century and more. Frith and his fellow studio photographers revisited locations many times down the years to update their views, compiling for us an enthralling and colourful pageant of British life and character.

We tend to think of Frith's sepia views of Britain as nostalgic, for most of us use them to conjure up memories of places in our own lives with which we have family associations. It often makes us forget that to Francis Frith they were records of daily life as it was actually being lived in the cities, towns and villages of his day. The Victorian age was one of great and often bewildering change for ordinary people,

and though the pictures evoke an impression of slower times, life was as busy and hectic as it is today.

We are fortunate that Frith was a photographer of the people, dedicated to recording the minutiae of everyday life. For it is this sheer wealth of visual data, the painstaking chronicle of changes in dress, transport, street layouts, buildings, housing, engineering and landscape that captivates us so much today. His remarkable images offer us a powerful link with the past and with the lives of our ancestors.

Today's Technology

Computers have now made it possible for Frith's many thousands of images to be accessed almost instantly. In the Frith archive today, each photograph is carefully 'digitised' then stored on a CD Rom. Frith archivists can locate a single photograph amongst thousands within seconds. Views can be catalogued and sorted under a variety of categories of place and content to the immediate benefit of researchers.

Inexpensive reference prints can be created for them at the touch of a mouse button, and a wide range of books and other printed materials assembled and published for a wider, more general readership - in the next twelve months over a hundred Frith local history titles will be published! The day-to-day workings of the archive are very different from how they were in Francis Frith's time: imagine the herculean task of sorting through eleven tons of glass negatives as Frith had to do to locate a

See Frith at www. francisfrith.co.uk

particular sequence of pictures! Yet the archive still prides itself on maintaining the same high standards of excellence laid down by Francis Frith, including the painstaking cataloguing and indexing of every view.

It is curious to reflect on how the internet now allows researchers in America and elsewhere greater instant access to the archive than Frith himself ever enjoyed. Many thousands of individual views can be called up on screen within seconds on one of the Frith internet sites, enabling people living continents away to revisit the streets of their ancestral home town, or view places in Britain where they have enjoyed holidays. Many overseas researchers welcome the chance to view special theme selections, such as transport, sports, costume and ancient monuments.

We are certain that Francis Frith would have heartily approved of these modern developments in imaging techniques, for he himself was always working at the very limits of Victorian photographic technology.

The Value of the Archive Today

Because of the benefits brought by the computer, Frith's images are increasingly studied by social historians, by researchers into genealogy and ancestry, by architects, town planners, and by teachers and schoolchildren involved in local history projects.

In addition, the archive offers every one of us an opportunity to examine the places where we and our families have lived and worked down the years. Highly successful in Frith's own era, the archive is now, a century and more on, entering a new phase of popularity.

The Past in Tune with the Future

Historians consider the Francis Frith Collection to be of prime national importance. It is the only archive of its kind remaining in private ownership and has been valued at a million pounds. However, this figure is now rapidly increasing as digital technology enables more and more people around the world to enjoy its benefits.

Francis Frith's archive is now housed in an historic timber barn in the beautiful village of Teffont in Wiltshire. Its founder would not recognize the archive office as it is today. In place of the many thousands of dusty boxes containing glass plate negatives and an all-pervading odour of photographic chemicals, there are now ranks of computer screens. He would be amazed to watch his images travelling round the world at unimaginable speeds through network and internet lines.

The archive's future is both bright and exciting. Francis Frith, with his unshakeable belief in making photographs available to the greatest number of people, would undoubtedly approve of what is being done today with his lifetime's work. His photographs, depicting our shared past, are now bringing pleasure and enlightenment to millions around the world a century and more after his death.

Yorkshire Living Memories
An Introduction

YORKSHIRE IS AS much a state of mind as a geographical place. Sometimes described as 'England's Texas', it has always prided itself on being the biggest - and best - of all the English counties. It still accounts for about an eighth of England's land area and about a tenth of its population. And 'Yorkshireness' is a characteristic of which the locals are also inordinately proud. It is marked by a certain stubbornness and strongly-held opinions, but above all it is characterised by the Tykes' enormous and unshakeable pride in the county of their birth.

Although the times have probably passed when a expatriate Yorkshire father would insist on his wife coming home for the birth of his children - just in case it was a boy who would then qualify to play cricket for the county - that pride in the 'Broad Acres' is still very evident in Yorkshire folk. It was never tested more when the mandarins of central government annexed part of the old East Riding in 1974 and called it 'Humberside'. It was not long before the brand-new signs announcing the new county were defaced by loyalists claiming it was still Yorkshire - they were enraged that part of their ancient county had been taken away from them. Let us be thankful that that unfortunate decision has since been reversed.

The old Yorkshire had been around for over 1,000 years. It takes its name from the ancient county town of York, which in turn gets its name from the Latinised Celtic Eboracum, meaning 'the estate of Eburos', to which was added the Anglo-Saxon 'wic' to create Eoforwic. This was rendered as Jorvik by the Vikings during the period of their occupation during the 10th and 11th centuries, and eventually it became Anglicised to York. It was those Viking Danes who first divided the huge county into the now-familiar 'ridings'. Originally, they were 'thridings' - or thirds - and they became the North, East and West Ridings before local government re-organisation in 1974. That ancient Danish and Norse heritage is still evident today in many Yorkshire place-names. In the Dales, words like 'thwaite', 'beck' and 'foss' all derive directly from the Old Norse language, while to the east, the Danish influence is marked by placenames ending in 'by' like Whitby and Hunmanby.

Roughly speaking, the North Riding stretched across from the famous Yorkshire Dales of the north Pennines to the North Sea via the North York Moors, and is mainly open moorland or pastoral farming country. This is the land of the Norse farmers, where isolated Pennine longhouse farms have sometimes been on the same site for a thousand years, and where sheep farming still predominates in the hills. The West Riding ran south-east from the Pennine foothills; it presents the archetypal Yorkshire scene of moorlands running down to narrow valleys, where terraced houses are dominated by grim mill and factory chimneys. The industrial cities of Leeds, Bradford, Huddersfield and Sheffield also formed part of the old West Riding, although the Sheffield area was known as South Yorkshire for a time in the 1990s. The East Riding, on the other hand, extended across the broad, fertile and mainly arable Vale of York to the great estuary of the Humber, with the curious 'tail' of Holderness leading out to Spurn Point.

Physically speaking, Yorkshire is dominated by the Pennines, that dissected chain of hills which run up the backbone of England from Derbyshire in the south to Northumberland in the north. Formed of sedimentary rocks - mainly limestone and millstone grit - around 350 million years ago, the Yorkshire Pennines are perhaps best known for their glorious dales. The succession of eastward-draining rivers - the Swale, Ure, Nidd, Wharfe, Aire, Calder and Don - all carve out beautiful valleys before emptying into the Humber or Ouse and eventually joining the North Sea. They form the basis of the lovely Yorkshire Dales, a National Park since 1954, and providing some of the most beautiful scenery in Britain. This was the landscape which prompted one of Yorkshire's most famous sons, the Bradford-born playwright J B Priestley, to say: 'In all my travels I've never seen a countryside to equal in beauty the Yorkshire Dales'. Each of the Dales has its own individual character, from the stern, northern marches of Swaledale, pitted with the evidence of centuries of lead mining, to the pastoral splendour of Wensleydale or Wharfedale, where lovely villages and venerable ruins such as Bolton Abbey (or Priory) and Barden Tower seem to grow naturally from the rocks. And the rock which adds so much to the character of the Dales is limestone, of which the poet W H Auden wrote in praise:

Mark these rounded slopes with their surface fragrance of thyme and beneath,
A secret system of caves and conduits: hear the springs
That spurt out everywhere with a chuckle,
Each filling a private pool for fish and carving
Its own little ravine whose cliffs entertain
The butterfly and the lizard.

The great scenic showplaces of the Dales, like Malham Cove, Gordale Scar and Kilnsey Crag, are all carved in limestone, and Auden's 'secret system of caves and conduits' include the fine showcaves of Ingleborough, White Scar and Stump Cross. Towering above them are some of the highest points in the Pennines, culminating in the famous Three Peaks of Yorkshire - Whernside, Ingleborough and Pen y Ghent - which dominate Ribblesdale; this is the only major dale which turns its back on the Humber and runs out through neighbouring Lancashire into the Irish Sea.

Further east in the old North Riding lies the old county of Cleveland and the North York Moors, another scenically-splendid part of the county which has also been a National Park for 50 years. The North York Moors are formed of Jurassic sandstones laid down between 210 and 145 million years ago, and they form a dissected plateau whose great glory is its mile after mile of purple-hued heather - a wonderful

sight in late summer. This is also Yorkshire's most impressive coastline, with great cliffs culminating in Boulby and interesting old fishing communities like those at Robin Hood's Bay, Staithes and Whitby, and a lovely interior with charming villages like Kirkbymoorside and Helmsley and great monastic ruins at Rosedale, Rievaulx and Byland.

The West Riding also has its scenic highlights, like the desolate moors of the South Pennines, personified by the Bronte family whose literary genius flowered in the village of Haworth; the lovely valleys of Hardcastle Crags and Luddenden; and the moors to the west of Sheffield - one of the only cities in Europe to have part of yet another National Park, the Peak District, within its boundaries. But this is mainly the 'dark Satanic mills' country of Blake, where the Industrial Revolution cities of Leeds, Bradford and Sheffield were founded on the fast-flowing rivers which originally gave power to their mills, and which are now gradually being restored to amenity and recreation. Leeds, Bradford, Halifax and Huddersfield were founded on the woollen and textile industries, of course, whereas Sheffield, Rotherham, Barnsley and Doncaster were until fairly recently great cities built on steel and coal. The great Yorkshire coalfield, sad to say now almost a thing of the past, provided many jobs and created many pit villages in the West and East Ridings, but today they are having to re-invent themselves in the light of a fast-changing world.

The old East Riding has always been a farming area, centred on the Plain of York and the ancient walled city of York which stands at its heart. Dominated by its magnificent Minster, York is famous for its chocolate and railways, but today its marvellous survival as a still mainly medieval city has marked it as one of the great tourist attractions of Britain. The chalk and limestone Howardian Hills run out to the sea at the wonderful chalk cliffs of Flamborough Head and Bempton, famous for their seabird colonies. Further up the coast, Yorkshire's seaside resorts of Scarborough and Filey are popular holiday places for the people of the West Riding industrial cities, while Kingston-upon-Hull on the Humber estuary, now safely back in Yorkshire again, is still an important and thriving Europe-facing seaport.

For the purposes of this book, Yorkshire has been divided into three again, but not strictly into the ancient former Ridings. First we head east towards the old East Riding including York and the lovely villages of the North York Moors and Cleveland. Then we move to photographs from the west and south of the county, including the industrial West Riding and South Yorkshire towns and cities. Finally we look at the Yorkshire Dales and the mainly moorland area of North Yorkshire.

The photographs mainly show us a Yorkshire when it was at its height as the industrial powerhouse of Britain. They show the great cities as cauldrons of industry and commerce, with many of the mills still in operation and the millworkers' cottages still in use for their original purpose, not as fashionable 'homes of character'. Out in the country, the scenes show us a Yorkshire before the invasion of the car, and many village streets appear to be empty of any form of traffic at all. The photographs show a more leisurely way of life when children could play safely in the street and the sight of a lorry or charabanc was still relatively unusual.

These Yorkshire Living Memories as recorded by the photographers of Francis Frith should stir many memories in Yorkshire people, who will recall those days of the not-so-distant past. But as always, it is the watching Pennines which form the backdrop to so many of the pictures, and they have not changed substantially; they still form that backbone to the landscape which meant so much to Priestley, Auden and so many others.

Eastern Yorkshire

AISLABY, THE VILLAGE C1955 A120001
A solitary car is parked outside the New Inn on the left in Aislaby, a small village near Whitby, just off the road that leads to Middlesbrough. The village is a pleasant mixture of stone-built and brick pantile-roofed houses.

ALDBROUGH ST JOHN, THE GREEN C1955 A121001
An impromptu cricket match takes place on The Green at Aldbrough St John on a glorious summer's day. This large village, just off the ancient Roman Road of Dere Street, later the Great North Road and the A1, lies near the Durham border west of Darlington.

APPLETON-LE-STREET, THE VILLAGE c1960 A128003
The quiet village street at Appleton-le-Street, west of Malton, shows little passing traffic outside the village pub. Note the pantiled roofs of the adjacent barns and sheds, a typical feature of the villages of East Yorkshire, where stone and slate is a rarity.

AMPLEFORTH, MAIN STREET c1955 A124024
The North Yorkshire village of Ampleforth is perhaps best known for its Roman Catholic boys' school situated to the east of the village, but this view shows the Main Street of the village itself, which lies on the southern edge of the Hambleton Hills.

FILEY, ON THE BEACH c1950 F23260
Lines of wind shelters adorn the beach at the popular Yorkshire coast resort of Filey. Once a fashionable beach accessory, they are seldom seen today, so perhaps it was windier in the Fifties! Filey Bay runs down from the prominent coastal feature of Filey Brig which juts out into the North Sea.

FILEY, LOWFIELD FARM CAMP, c1965 F23135

Here we see the modest wooden buildings of the Lowfield Farm Camp, which was a predecessor of the giant holiday camp near Hunmanby which now dominates Filey Bay. The caravans have been replaced by permanent chalets and a huge entertainment complex, which is open for most of the year.

FYLINGDALES, THE EARLY WARNING SYSTEM c1960 F91002

The gigantic white 'golf balls' of the Fylingdales Early Warning System were a landmark on the eastern side of the North York Moors National Park for many years, before being replaced in the 1990s with a truncated pyramid which served the same function. The end of Communism has made these intrusive symbols of the Cold War virtually redundant.

GREAT AYTON, HIGH STREET c1965 G112031
Great Ayton is one of Cleveland's prettiest villages, and was the scene of the upbringing and education of Captain James Cook, the famous 18th-century world explorer. The High Street runs alongside the River Leven, where the young Cook must have played as a youth.

GREEN HAMMERTON, MAIN STREET c1960 G116011
Whitewashed houses and pantiled roofs characterise this photograph of the deserted Main Street of Green Hammerton, a small village in the Vale of York and on Roman Dere Street, just off the main A59 Harrogate to York road. It was the home of Thomas 'Alleluia Tommy' Segmore, a famous Methodist preacher.

HELMSLEY
The Square c1955 H201045
The ancient, ivy-covered Black Swan Hotel dominates this view of The Square at Helmsley, the attractive castle-crowned capital of the North York Moors National Park. In the background is the pinnacled tower of the parish church of All Saints, largely rebuilt in 1867.

Detail of H201045

HOVINGHAM
The Village c1965 H217023
The pretty estate village of Hovingham, in the Vale of Pickering, is famous for its lime trees which shade the entrance to Hovingham Hall, built about 1760 by Thomas Worsley, Surveyor General to William III. A pleasing mixture of architectural styles is seen in this photograph of the centre of the village.

Detail of H217023

HUSTHWAITE, EAST VIEW C1955 H221012

Until recently, Husthwaite, on the western edge of the Hambleton Hills near Easingwold, was known as the Orchard Village because of its abundance of apple, pear and plum orchards. The village of mellow Victorian and Edwardian houses has not changed much since this photograph was taken.

HUTTONS AMBO, THE SWING BRIDGE C1960 H224013

This elegant little suspension or 'swing bridge' over the River Derwent is a pleasing feature of the Plain of York village of Huttons Ambo, near Malton. Hutton was put on the map by the coming of the York to Scarborough railway, which follows the course of the Derwent.

KIRKBYMOORSIDE, HIGH MARKET PLACE 1951 K130009
The cobble-edged wide Market Place of Kirkbymoorside, on the edge of the North York Moors, still holds its market every Wednesday, just as it has done since medieval times. The ivy-clad King's Head public house, on the right, is a popular local hostelry, although the gallows-type pub sign out in the street has long gone.

LANGTON, THE VILLAGE c1965 L175009
The cottages of Langton, near Malton, still cluster around the village green, as they did when this photograph was taken. Note the sturdy, gritstone-built Georgian cottages with their uniformly white-painted doors and windows.

MALTON
THE MARKET PLACE c1965 M141018
The Norman tower of St Michael's parish church watches over the busy Market Place of Malton, filled with cars in this picture. Malton stands at the junction of many roads above the Derwent Valley south of the North York Moors, and has been an important market centre since the Middle Ages.

NORTHALLERTON
NORTH END c1960 N75002

The Highways Department had made a fine job of the flowerbeds of this roundabout at the North End of Northallerton, the busy little town on the River Wiske on the western edge of the North York Moors. In the background on the left is the parish church of All Saints, a stately building restored in 1884 but with a fine 15th-century tower.

PICKERING, POTTER HILL C1955 P156087

Now known as the 'Gateway to the Moors', Pickering is a small market town still served by the steam trains of the North York Moors Railway. This view of Potter Hill shows the classical façade of the Primitive Methodist Chapel, built in 1885, on the left.

REIGHTON, SEA VIEW STORES C1965 R239068

A holidaying family does a bit of window shopping at the Sea View Stores on the front at Reighton, while a dog watches curiously on to the left. Reighton is a small resort on Filey Bay, and Reighton Sands are still justly famous for their bathing.

ROBIN HOOD'S BAY, THE BAY HOTEL c1965 R41052

Robin Hood's Bay is one of many beautiful villages which cluster around the steep-sided coves where the North York Moors reach the North Sea. At the time when this picture was taken, horses and carts like that in the centre of the photograph were still a common sight outside the Bay Hotel, overlooking the sea front. In the foreground, Mum and Dad watch over their children who are sitting in a small fishing boat.

ROSEDALE ABBEY, THE VILLAGE c1955 R245015

The chapel is prominent on the right in this view of the small hamlet of Rosedale Abbey, which sits in the heart of Rosedale on the southern edge of the North York Moors, seen filling the background. It was a boom town during the 19th-century iron-mining era, and takes its name from the remains of a 12th-century Cistercian nunnery now built into the parish church.

SCARBOROUGH
South Bay c1960 S71103
The extensive remains of 12th-century Scarborough Castle crown the headland in the background of this summer time view of Scarborough's South Beach. Scarborough's sandy beaches are still as popular now with northern holidaymakers, who still throng to the seaside town for the donkey rides, candy floss and sticks of rock as they did 40 years ago.

Detail of S71103

STAITHES, HIGH STREET c1955 S176090

The narrow cobbled streets of Staithes still wind down to the North Sea just as they did in the 1950s. Captain James Cook was employed here as a grocer's apprentice, perhaps in a shop like that on the right of this photograph, before he made his name as the discoverer of Australia.

SWINTON, MAIN STREET c1960 S243021

The small hamlet of Swinton, west of Malton on the B1257, above the wide valley of the River Rye, was completely deserted when the Frith photographer called on a summer's day. The garages on both the right and left of the photograph were both open and waiting for passing trade, but none seemed to be evident.

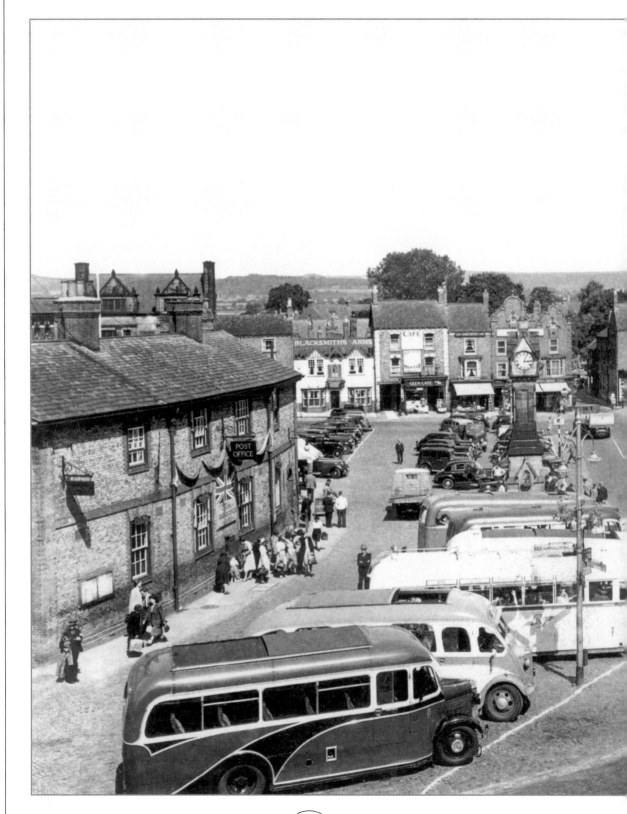

THIRSK

MARKET PLACE c1955 T306030
It is Market Day in the busy little town of Thirsk, standing at the foot of the Hambleton Hills, halfway between York and Darlington. Thirsk has always been an important stopping place on the old Great North Road, and the Golden Fleece Inn, on the extreme right of the picture, was a coaching inn where horses were changed. Today, Thirsk is the heart of James Herriot Country, and the actual vet in the stories, Alf Wight, was married in St Mary's Church here in 1941.

THORNTON DALE, THE FORGE c1955 T139060

When this photograph was taken, the pantiled old forge at Thornton Dale on the A170 east of Pickering had already diversified into pottery, postcards and gifts, as well as the more traditional metalwork. But the horse and carriage parked outside show there was still a demand from the equestrian trade.

WASS, MAIN STREET c1955 W580001

Here we see the entrance to the charming little village of Wass, which lies in a shallow valley under the wooded southern escarpment of the Hambleton Hills, seen in the background. Note the pantiles on the roofs of the cottages on the left, typical of the villages on the eastern side of Yorkshire.

TOPCLIFFE, LONG STREET c1955 T138017
Seen from its modern bypass on the A168 trunk road south of Thirsk, Topcliffe looks like a modern village of new housing estates. But this 1950s view of Long Street shows some of the older, Georgian cottages at the top end of the village, where annual horse and sheep fairs were held until the late 1960s.

WHITBY, THE UPPER HARBOUR c1955 W81040

This view of the Upper Harbour in the ancient port of Whitby situated where the River Esk runs into the North Sea has hardly changed since the 1950s. It shows the headland of the East Cliff in the background, with the parish Church of St Mary's, and the skeletal remains of the 13th-century Benedictine Abbey.

WHITBY, THE STEPS TO THE PARISH CHURCH c1955 W81045

Another view of Whitby, this time showing the Upper Harbour beyond the causeway which leads to the famous 199 steps which lead up to St Mary's Church and the Abbey. The Abbey was founded in AD657 by St Hilda; it was the setting for Bram Stoker's classic horror novel, 'Dracula'.

YORK, LOW PETERGATE c1960 Y12060
Low Petergate is one of the many narrow side-streets which lead up towards the towers of York Minster, seen in the centre background. Note the overhanging eaves of the shops and houses, characteristic of the medieval street lay-out of York which is still unchanged today.

YORK, BOOTHAM BAR c1950 Y12008

Low Petergate (seen in the previous photograph) and High Petergate run up to Bootham Bar, one of York's still surviving medieval gates in the city walls, and to the Thirsk road out of the city. Again, the pinnacled twin western towers of the Minster can be seen in the background.

YORK, MONK BAR c1955 Y12044

Monk Bar is one of the finest gates in the city walls and the closest to the Minster on Goodramgate. It is vaulted on three floors, and still has a working portcullis. The road passes through the walls between the two arches shown in this photograph, and the walk around the surviving walls of York is still one of the finest ways to see the city.

YORK, THE SHAMBLES c1962 Y12062

Perhaps the best-known of York's medieval streets is The Shambles, seen here looking towards Pavement, and virtually unchanged today. The word 'shambles' comes from the Old English 'shamel', which means a slaughterhouse, so presumably this was once a street of butchers. Today, the delightful mixture of medieval half-timbered and Georgian houses are mostly craft and antique shops, catering for the tourist.

West & South Yorkshire

ADDINGHAM
THE CHURCH c1955 A118010
This scene of the parish church of St Peter at Addingham, standing in its walled churchyard on the village green and reached by a stone bridge over the beck, has not changed substantially since this photograph was taken. A former church on the site is said to have been a place of refuge for Archbishop Wulfere of York as he escaped from the marauding Danes.

BARNSLEY, AERIAL VIEW C1966 B333021
This aerial view of the South Yorkshire town of Barnsley centres on the imposing white stone Town Hall with its monolithic central clock tower. Much has changed today, with many of the terraced houses of miners from the former South Yorkshire coalfield now swept away and replaced by modern shopping and office blocks.

BAILDON, FROM THE BANK c1960 B332019
The steep slopes of The Bank provide a grandstand view of Baildon, a typical Pennine town standing on the edge of Baildon Moor, famous for its enigmatic prehistoric 'cup and ring'-marked stones. In the background can be seen the tower of the parish church of St John, built in 1848.

BAWTRY, THE MARKET PLACE c1965 B334027
This view shows a virtually-deserted Market Place at Bawtry, with a 'half-timbered' Morris Minor prominently parked by the old Buttercross. Bawtry was once an important coaching stop on the old Great North Road, where horses were changed on the journey north to Scotland. It had also been an important port on the River Idle since Roman times, linking to the Humber.

BINGLEY, MAIN STREET c1955 B98019

You would take your life in your hands if you tried to take this view looking south up the A650 Bradford-Skipton road in the centre of the Airedale town of Bingley today. In the mid-1950s, however, there were still horses and carts in the street (centre), and motorists still had time to read the advertising hoardings visible on the building on the left. The lane off to the right leads to the parish church of All Saints.

BLAXTON, BLUE BELL INN CORNER c1955 B340004

A landmark on the Bawtry-Thorne road, the Blue Bell Inn stands at the crossroads of the Doncaster-Epworth road in the heart of the low-lying Hatfield Moors, close to the RAF station at Finningley. Two mobile cycle-towed workshops, owned probably by a knife grinder or a similar tradesmen, stand outside the inn.

BOLSTERSTONE, THE VILLAGE FROM FOLDERINGS LANE c1955 B341001
The ridgetop village of Bolsterstone stands at nearly 1,000 feet above the sea on the edge of the Peak District moors north-west of Sheffield. It is a pleasant, gritstone village, famous for its choir, which often sings in the pinnacled parish church, seen peeping above the roofs of the village in the background.

BRADFORD, THE CARTWRIGHT MEMORIAL HALL c1950 B173024
The Cartwright Memorial Hall in Lister Park, Bradford, built during the time of Bradford's pre-eminence as one of the major woollen manufacturing towns of the world, now houses one of the city's best museums and art galleries. There are important collections of 19th- and early 20th-century paintings inside, including many by the Pre-Raphaelite Brotherhood. More recent acquisitions include paintings by Bradford's own David Hockney.

CAWTHORNE, TAYLOR HILL c1955 C259006

There was no traffic on Taylor Hill, Cawthorne when this picture was taken, and the parked car was the only sign of life, apart from the two pedestrians on the right. Cawthorne is a village on the edge of the Pennines west of Barnsley on the Holmfirth road in the valley of the River Dearne.

CLAYTON WEST, LONG LANE c1955 C262005

Clayton West was typical of many South Yorkshire coalfield villages in the 1950s, when this photograph was taken. The village was a mixture of a rural and industrial landscapes; to the left, corn is stacked up in stooks ready for harvesting, while to the right, behind the houses, a chimney and the huge shape of the spoil tip of the pit which gave the village its name breaks the horizon.

CLECKHEATON
The Green c1965 C263004
Cleckheaton is another former textile town, five miles south of Bradford, which has had to find a new role during the late 20th century. This photograph of The Green shows the mock-Gothic Martin's Bank in the centre of the town.

Detail of C263004

COLLINGHAM, POST OFFICE CORNER c1950 C265027
Cyclists were still quite safe to meander along in the middle of the road when this photograph was taken in Collingham, near Wetherby. Collingham stands on the River Wharfe on a major route north from Leeds, and was originally the site of a Roman settlement.

CONISBROUGH, THE CASTLE c1965 C152010
A new visitor centre now marks the entrance to Conisbrough Castle, one of the best-preserved Norman castles in the country. The tall, cylindrical keep with its six massive buttresses was built about 1180 by Henry II's half-brother, Hamelin Plantagenet, and still comes as a surprise as you approach this small South Yorkshire village on the A630 south west of Doncaster.

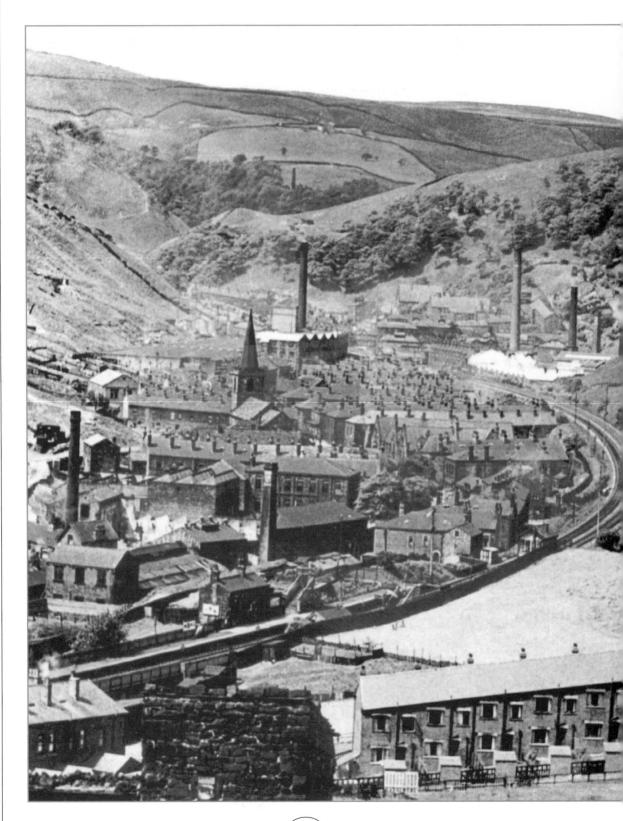

CORNHOLME
GENERAL VIEW c1955 C268004
An archetypal Pennine industrial landscape is presented in this view of Cornholme, in the deep valley of the River Calder between Burnley and Todmorden. The chimneys of the textile mills fill the valley bottom, alongside the winding railway line and grim terraces of the millworkers' cottages. Above them, the moors watch over, unchanged.

CRAGG VALE, GENERAL VIEW c1955 C272001
Cragg Vale, seen here from above the village, was a remote hamlet above the Calder Valley in the 18th century, when it was the base of a notorious gang of counterfeiters known as the 'Cragg Vale Coiners'. Led by David Hartley, they clipped the edges of gold guineas and forged new coins from the metal.

CRAGG VALE, ST JOHN'S PARISH CHURCH c1955 C272002
The pinnacled Victorian Parish Church of St John, Cragg Vale, with its crowded graveyard, looks down the isolated, wooded valley where the coiners once operated, far from the eyes of the law and authority.

DENBY DALE, HIGH STREET C1955 D98008

The viaduct which carries the main Sheffield-Leeds railway line dominates this view of the High Street of the South Yorkshire town of Denby Dale. Denby Dale is perhaps most famous for its gargantuan meat and potato pies, first baked to celebrate the recovery of King George III from one of his many bouts of illness.

DEWSBURY, THE TOWN HALL C1960 D100002

This 1960s photograph shows how uncomfortably the Victorian Town Hall at Dewsbury sat with the recently-built modernistic shop and office block opposite. Dewsbury was the centre of the 'shoddy' woollen industry, which re-used old woollen items to make heavy woollens such as blankets and military uniforms.

EAST KESWICK, STOCK'S HILL c1955 E77006
The recent history of the ancient village of East Keswick is inextricably linked with the fortunes of the nearby 'big house' of Harewood. Many of the villagers worked for the Lascelles family before the village was sold off to pay death duties at about the time this picture of Stock's Hill was taken. Note the stone-faced telephone box (centre right).

ELLAND, GENERAL VIEW c1960 E79019
Another typical West Yorkshire mill town, Elland lies on a bend in the Calder Valley and is still dominated, as in this photograph, by large woollen mills. It is perhaps most famous as the home of the Gannex raincoat, much favoured by Prime Minister Harold Wilson, who hailed from nearby Huddersfield.

FINNINGLEY, THE POND c1955 F67001
Once many villages were clustered around the village pond, and this shot of Finningley in South Yorkshire shows it was no exception. The village is perhaps best known for the RAF base nearby, now closed down and awaiting redevelopment.

GOLDTHORPE, THE MINERS' WELFARE HALL c1960 G110001
The 'Miners' Welfare' was the community and cultural centre for many South Yorkshire and other coal mining villages. But not many were as grand as this one at Goldthorpe, near Barnsley, built in 1923 with Tuscan-ordered entrance columns and elegant, classical proportions.

HALIFAX
THE TOWN CENTRE c1955 H9011
At its height in the 19th and early 20th century, Halifax was the greatest of the textile towns of West Yorkshire, a centre for woollen manufacture and clothing, larger even than Leeds or Bradford. The Victorian wealth of the town is shown in the fine buildings in this view of the main shopping street, with the Halifax Building Society, which started here, prominent on the right.

HAWORTH, MAIN STREET 1958 H194028
The Bronte industry, founded in this pretty, cobble-streeted West Yorkshire town after the famous literary family made the Parsonage their home in 1820, was already well under way, if this 1950s photograph is anything to go by. The Post Office (left) also advertises Bronte books and postcards, while the Bronte Guest House is visible behind the antiques shop (right centre).

HECKMONDWIKE, MARKET STREET c1955 H199007
The pavements of Market Street were crowded with pram-pushing mothers shopping for the week's provisions. Another of the region's many woollen manufacturing towns, Heckmondwike still exhibits the same no-nonsense, down-to-earth air which characterises this part of the county.

HECKMONDWIKE, THE MARKET SQUARE c1955 H199008
Busy market stalls cluster around the Victorian clock-topped monument in the Market Square of Heckmondwike on a summer afternoon. The Red Lion public house is on the right, while the factory chimney in the background is a reminder of the town's industrial base.

HEMSWORTH, THE PARISH CHURCH c1955 H204003
The parish church of St Helen stands on a slight rise above the centre of the former coal mining town of Hemsworth, near Wakefield. The church was extensively remodelled in 1867, but parts of the imposing building date from the 13th century, when Hemsworth was a prosperous market town.

HEPTONSTALL, THE TWO PARISH CHURCHES c1965 H205001
This view from Horsehold overlooks the wooded Calder Valley; it shows Heptonstall's two parish churches, one in the valley at Mytholm and the other on the hill above (centre background) in the actual hilltop village of Heptonstall. The view shows a typical West Yorkshire industrial landscape of mills; these ones were originally powered by the fast-flowing streams of Colden Clough.

HOLMFIRTH, VICTORIA SQUARE c1955 H212004
The long-running TV comedy, 'Last of the Summer Wine', had not put Holmfirth on the tourist map when this photograph of main square was taken. But even before Compo and Co arrived, Holmfirth had achieved fame as the home of Bamforth's comic postcards, and as the scene of the earliest awakenings of the British film industry.

HORBURY, HIGH STREET c1955 H214002

Horbury, three miles south-west of Wakefield, was once one of the busiest railway junctions in the country; hence, perhaps, the absence of any form of traffic in the High Street in this photograph. A three-wheeler delivery van waits for the latest edition outside the offices of the 'Horbury Observer' newspaper on the left.

HORBURY, CLUNTERGATE c1955 H214017

Cluntergate is one of the main roads leading out from the centre of Horbury, whose main claim to fame is that it was the birthplace of the famous 18th-century architect always, but erroneously, known as 'John Carr of York'. He is buried in the crypt of the parish church of St Peter and St Leonard, which he designed and built himself.

HORSFORTH, NEW ROAD c1965 H118050
Horsforth is now not much more than a suburb of nearby Leeds, but when this photograph was taken, it still retained its separate, village character. The town was founded on a ford over the River Aire, near Kirkstall Forge, where the monks of Kirkstall Abbey once smelted iron ore.

HOYLAND, HIGH STREET c1960 H218027
Hoyland, properly Hoyland Nether, is a large former coal mining village between Sheffield and Barnsley. This view shows the High Street devoid of traffic, with the shops of Melias Ltd, grocers, and Storey Cooper, drapers, with their summer awnings out.

HOYLAND, ELSECAR COLLIERY c1960 H218020

Elsecar was one of the many collieries which formerly existed in the South Yorkshire coalfield around the village of Hoyland. The winding wheels of two pitheads are visible, with a tall chimney of what was probably a coking plant in between.

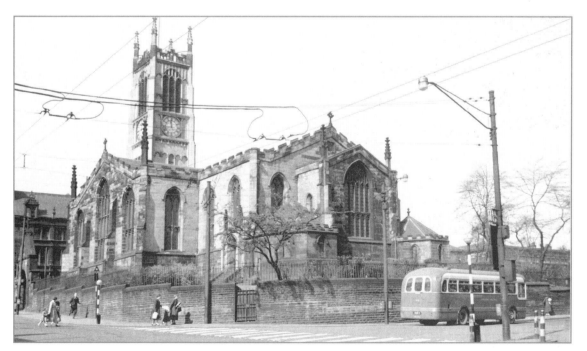

HUDDERSFIELD, THE PARISH CHURCH c1960 H151015

The parish church of St Peter at Huddersfield was built on a Norman foundation, but was extensively restored and remodelled by J P Pritchett of York in 1836, in the Victorian Gothic style.

HUDDERSFIELD
NEW STREET 1957 H151010
The bustling town of Huddersfield, like so many other Pennine towns, was founded on the wealth won from the 19th-century explosion in the worsted and woollen industries. When this photograph was taken, with the white painted Commercial Hotel on the left, there were still trams running up and down the town's streets.

ILLINGWORTH, THE TALBOT INN AND THE CHURCH c1960 I60020

The parish church stands on the hill. Illingworth was at the time of this photograph a village on the edge of the Pennines north of Halifax, but is now a suburb of the city. The handsome Talbot Inn at the foot of the hill recalls a prominent local family. The inn sign, seen on the extreme right of this photograph, shows a foxhound, perhaps indicating the family's hobby.

OGDEN, THE RESERVOIR c1960 O144005

The steep valleys, or cloughs, which run off the foothills of the Pennines were often utilised by Victorian water engineers for the construction of reservoirs to provide drinking water for the burgeoning industrial cities in the plains below. Ogden Reservoir, north-west of Illingworth in West Yorkshire, dammed the waters of the Hebble Brook, and is now backed by the wind farm on Ovenden Moor.

KEIGHLEY

Skipton Road c1955 K60002

Panama-hatted Tom Roe, 'Dealer in Worn-out Horses' (perhaps a grand name for a rag and bone man), clip-clops his way down the Skipton Road through Keighley. To his left, a group of schoolchildren mill around waiting for their school bus, while opposite, the gleaming white building of the Picture House awaits its cinemagoers.

Detail of K60002

KIPPAX, HIGH STREET c1965 K72044
The unusual placename of Kippax, a village to the east of Leeds, comes from the Saxon, and means 'Cyppa's ash tree'. Perhaps the Old Tree Inn, on the right of the photograph, echoes that ancient foundation. There is a fine Norman church here, built on the site of a Saxon predecessor.

KIRKBURTON, NORTH ROAD c1955 K75023

Many Pennine woollen towns had strong Liberal leanings, and prominent in this photograph of Kirkburton, near Huddersfield, is the tall four-storey building of the Liberal Club, a centre of local community affairs and politics. On the left is the town's Post Office, converted from a private house.

LEEDS, THE HEADROW AND THE TOWN HALL c1955 L28004

The magnificent many-pillared clock tower of Leeds Town Hall, opened by Queen Victoria in 1858, dominates this view of The Headrow, one of the city's most important thoroughfares. Leeds Town Hall, designed by the Hull architect Cuthbert Broderick, has been described as one of the best examples of the Classical revival style in England.

MELTHAM, HOLMFIRTH ROAD c1955 M144016

The old flaming torch sign (left) marks the approach to the village school in Holmfirth Road, Meltham, another Pennine edge town founded on the textile industry. On the other side of the road, people queue for the Huddersfield and District bus which has just arrived and will later call at Scholes, on the other side of Holmfirth.

MILNSBRIDGE, MARKET STREET c1955 M146013

Milnsbridge is now a suburb to the west of Huddersfield, and this picture shows its history as yet another typical Pennine mill town, with the imposing mill buildings filling the skyline, and the railway viaduct in the background.

MYTHOLMROYD, VIEW FROM SCOUT ROAD c1955 M151005

There could not be anywhere more northern-sounding than Mytholmroyd, the woollen village crammed into the bottom of the Calder Valley west of Halifax. The name means 'the clearing where the waters meet', the waters being the Calder and the Cragg Brook. Prominent in this view from Scout Road, which leads up through Hathershelf Scout Wood, south east of the village, is the Moderna Blanket Factory.

NEW ROSSINGTON, THE COLLIERY, WEST END LANE c1955 N73005

The winding gear and smoke-belching chimney of the colliery dominate the end of the council houses of West End Lane, New Rossington, at a time when coal was still king in South Yorkshire.

NEW ROSSINGTON, KING AVENUE c1955 N73006

New Rossington, a village lying to the south of Doncaster, was created when the colliery was sunk into the rich South Yorkshire coalfield. It lies adjacent to the older village of Rossington, but took over in importance when mining became the local industry, gaining its own branch of the Doncaster Co-operative Society, seen on the right.

NORMANTON, HIGH STREET c1955 N159009

This view shows a virtually-deserted High Street in the undistinguished former colliery town of Normanton, three miles north of Wakefield in South Yorkshire. Normanton is thought to have Viking origins - its name means 'the town of the Northmen' - and earthworks nearby may be of Roman origin.

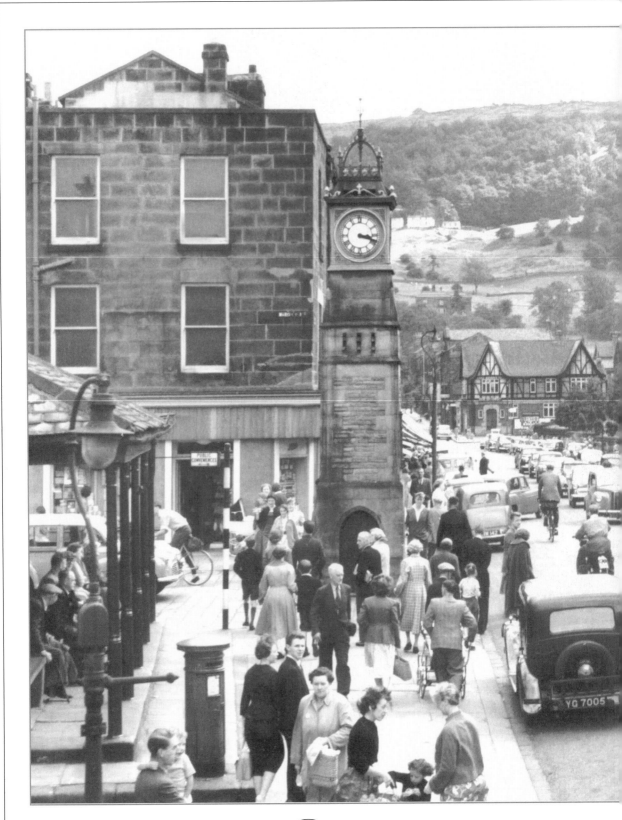

OTLEY, KIRKGATE c1960 O49040
What a contrast to the previous photograph this view of Kirkgate, Otley is. The lovely market town lies at the entrance to Wharfedale. The bustle of what must have been a market day is evident in the thronging crowds around the clock-tower and the busy road. In the background are the hills which lead up to Otley's most famous landmark, The Chevin.

OUGHTIBRIDGE, CROSS ROADS c1960 O50012

The steep road leading down to the bridge over the River Don at Oughtibridge, north of Sheffield, leads the eye to the steel works across the river. Opposite the Cock Inn (left) stands the tiny village Post Office, with a pensioner eyeing the photographer suspiciously.

PONTEFRACT, MARKET PLACE 1964 P155029

Famous for its liquorice 'cakes' or sweets, Pontefract is an ancient market town at the junction of the Rivers Aire and Calder, south of Castleford. This photograph looks down the length of the Market Place, with the white columns of the Market Hall, built in 1860, prominent on the right.

RAWMARSH, THE PARISH CHURCH AND THE MARKET c1965 R234008
The pinnacles of the parish church in the background overlook the covered stalls of Rawmarsh Market. Rawmarsh
is a former colliery town north of Rotherham in South Yorkshire.

RIPPONDEN, THE VILLAGE 1962 R242013

Standing high in the Pennines on Yorkshire's border with Lancashire, Ripponden has been an important settlement on the River Ryburn, but made its name from the wool trade in the 19th century and before. This view shows the centre of the village near the junction of the Elland Road.

ROTHERHAM, THE TOWN HALL c1955 R60010

The grimly-austere gritstone buildings of Rotherham Town Hall's Welfare and Health Department are typical of the South Yorkshire town's 'muck and brass' reputation. It was founded on the wealth of the coal industry, and although that has largely vanished now, Rotherham retains its air of gritty independence.

ROYSTON, THE TOWN CENTRE c1960 R248023

Royston is another former colliery town north of Barnsley. This view of the cross-roads in the centre of the town shows how free from congestion the roads were at the time of this photograph, before the days of universal car ownership.

SHEFFIELD, THE TOWN HALL c1965 S108241

This view across what is now known as the Peace Gardens towards the mock-Gothic spires of Sheffield's Town Hall has not changed significantly since this photograph was taken. Steps now lead down to the Gardens, which have recently been converted to include water features and fountains.

SHEFFIELD, VIEW OF ST PETER'S CHURCH c1965 S108188
The simple spire of St Peter's Church, Sheffield is typical of many such post-modern churches, which were built as large new council housing estates were erected in the suburbs of 'the Steel City', now the fifth largest in England.

SHIPLEY, COMMERCIAL STREET c1955 S122006
Shipley, three miles north-west of Bradford, in the valley of the River Aire, is a busy town on the A65 Skipton Road. A point of interest in this photograph is the Farm Shop in the centre of the picture, showing that such agricultural diversification is not such a new thing.

SILSDEN, TANNERY CORNER c1955 S307005

Tannery Corner, in the Airedale village of Silsden, takes it name from the tannery of William Laycock and Son, seen in the right background of this picture. A local resident enjoys the summer sun on the bench beneath the roadsign, which points the way to neighbouring Steeton.

SKELMANTHORPE, COMMERCIAL ROAD c1955 S309006

Two chums (right) march down Commercial Road, in the South Yorkshire colliery village of Skelmanthorpe. Skelmanthorpe, between Holmfirth and Barnsley, is a village of Scandinavian descent, as witnessed by its name, which means 'Skelmer's village in a valley'.

SOUTH KIRKBY, THE GREEN C1965 S560010
The newly-cut village green at South Kirkby, near Hemsworth, gives a neat, urban appearance to this former West Yorkshire mining village. In the background is the Travellers Inn, a popular village hostelry.

SLAITHWAITE, THE VILLAGE c1960 S310004
Locals pronounce Slaithwaite 'Slawit', and this bustling village in the valley of the River Calder four miles south-west of Huddersfield is another one with Norse origins. Its name means 'the clearing where the sloes grow'. Note the overhead tram wires.

SPROTBROUGH, THE VILLAGE c1960 S179005
The commanding tower of the village parish church overlooks the quiet South Yorkshire village of Sprotbrough, now divorced from the neighbouring town of Doncaster by the busy A1M motorway. The village stores stand on the left of the photograph.

STEETON, THE TOWER c1955 S321003

Although it is set in the heart of the largely industrialised Aire Valley, Steeton retains its air of rural tranquillity. This view is of The Tower, a crenellated gateway to the 17th-century High Hall, the village manor house. There is also a Low Hall at Steeton.

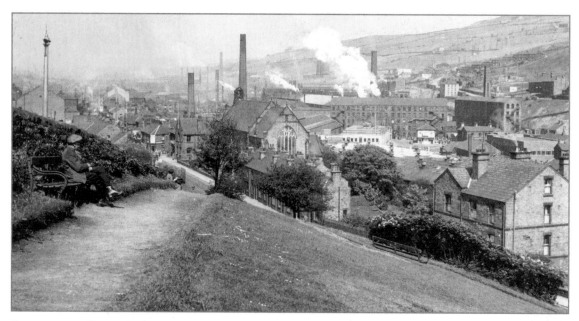

STOCKSBRIDGE, FROM THE CLOCK TOWER c1955 S324018

A retired steelman looks across the industrial landscape of Stocksbridge, the steel-making town in the valley of the River Don between Sheffield and Penistone, on the edge of the Pennine moors. Now bypassed by the A616, Stocksbridge has been 'cleaned up'; it no longer has the constant pall of smoke hanging over it, as it did when this photograph was taken.

SWALLOWNEST, WORKSOP ROAD c1955 S330009

Swallownest is a charmingly-named former mining village on the outskirts of Rotherham. This view shows the Swallownest Inn (centre) next to the petrol station with its old fashioned Esso petrol pumps.

THORNE, KING STREET c1955 T303023

Thorne was an important inland port linking the South Yorkshire coalfield and the River Don with the Aire and Calder Navigation and the River Humber via the Stainforth and Keadby Canal. Note the abundant cigarette advertising in the shops in King Street, and the steam roller at the bottom of the street (centre).

THORNE, THE CANAL c1955 T303012

A large barge bound for the Humber makes its stately way down the Stainforth and Keadby Canal at Thorne. The canal linked the River Don with the Humber, which it joined near the neighbouring village of Keadby.

TODMORDEN, CHURCH STREET c1955 T137001

For many years, Todmorden (or 'Tod' as it is always known locally) straddled the border between Yorkshire and Lancashire, and this busy, bustling little town has always had a foot in both camps, although it is now fiercely Yorkshire. This view in Church Street looks up to the elegant spire of the Victorian parish church.

TODMORDEN, THE TOWN HALL c1955 T137002
Todmorden Town Hall, built in 1870, once stood on the border between Yorkshire and Lancashire, a fact reflected in the carvings in the pediment frieze on its classical front, shown here: there are bales of cotton on the western (Lancashire) side and wool on the eastern (Yorkshire) side. Pevsner compared this fine Town Hall to that of Birmingham.

WAKEFIELD

CROSS SQUARE c1953 W464001
The abundance of Union Jacks and other flags in this view of Wakefield indicates that the photograph was taken in 1953, the year of Queen Elizabeth II's Coronation. A sign across the street advertises the Great Yorkshire Show held in early July, and the Coronation was on 2 June. In the background is the spire of the 14th-century cathedral church of All Saints.

WAKEFIELD, WOOD STREET c1953 W464005
More evidence of Coronation flags and bunting is shown in this view of Wood Street, Wakefield, looking up towards the clock tower of the Town Hall, built in 1880 in the French Gothic style by T E Collcutt, the architect of London's Savoy Hotel. Further up is the Mechanics' Institution, or Institute of Literature and Science, now housing the Wakefield Museum.

WADWORTH, THE SQUARE c1965 W218007
The White Hart Inn at Wadworth, south of Doncaster, was once an important stopping place on the old Great North Road. Now it is bypassed by the A1M motorway, and some of its rural serenity has been recovered. Note the maypole outside the inn.

WALSDEN

The Church and the Lock c1960

Walsden is a former woollen town in the Calder Gap between Yorkshire and Lancashire, just to the south of Todmorden. The Rochdale Canal, seen here in the foreground, runs through the valley, and brought jobs and prosperity to the town. The spire of the parish church watches over the town school in the background.

WALSDEN

The Village c1960

A typical Pennine farmstead, sheltered by a sycamore and standing on the edge of the moors, lies on the outskirts of Walsden. Note the well-kept drystone walls in the lane which leads up to the farm and then onto the moors, where there is evidence of stone quarrying in the hillside in the distance.

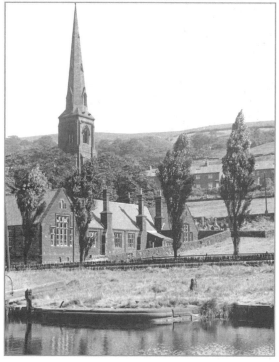

WALSDEN, THE CHURCH AND THE LOCK c1960 W219003

WALSDEN, THE VILLAGE c1960 W219002

WENTWORTH WOODHOUSE C1965 W233006

Wentworth Woodhouse is one of England's forgotten treasures, four miles north-west of Rotherham. This great, 18th-century Palladian mansion has a 600-foot frontage, one of the longest in England, and was the home of the Fitzwilliam family; it later became a teachers' training college.

WOODHOUSE, THE CROSS AND THE OLD CROSS DAGGERS C1960 W517003

The restored cross in the centre of Woodhouse, a South Yorkshire village east of Sheffield, stands on an ancient stepped base and now features a sundial and a weathervane. Opposite is the equally ancient Old Cross Daggers public house, one of the oldest buildings in the village.

WORTLEY, THE STORES AND POST OFFICE c1960 W232008
Converted from a Georgian private house, the Village Stores and Post Office was the communal centre of the former West Yorkshire village of Wortley, which is now not much more than a suburb of the city of Leeds.

YEADON, HIGH STREET c1965 Y37006
The hillside town of Yeadon lies to the north of Bradford, and is today perhaps most famous as the site of the Leeds-Bradford Airport. This photograph looks up the High Street towards the town's bus station. A rarity today would be the pork butchers' shop, on the right with the pram outside.

Northern Yorkshire and the Dales

APPLETREEWICK
Main Street c1955 A129003
We are looking down the Main Street of the charmingly-
named hamlet of Appletreewick in Wharfedale, with the
prominent 1,550ft fell of Simon's Seat in the background.
Known as 'Aptrick' to its residents, Appletreewick was once a
centre for lead mining, but farming and tourism are the dual
economies of today.

◆

ARKENGARTHDALE, THE CB HOTEL c1960 A130003

The white-painted CB Hotel in remote Arkengarthdale recalls the initials of Charles Bathurst, the 19th-century lead mining master who owned the circular powder house of the CB Smelt Mill nearby. Further up the Arkle Beck is the pub-less hamlet which glories in the entirely-inappropriate name of Booze.

ASKRIGG, THE MARKET CROSS c1955 A76003

Three-storied 18th-century town houses, including the bow-windowed front of the Sykes Temperance Hotel, line the Market Place of Askrigg, a pleasant village in Upper Wensleydale. The ancient stone market cross watches over the village as it has for over 500 years.

BAINBRIDGE, GENERAL VIEW c1955 B5005

Just down in the dale from Askrigg, on the banks of the River Ure, stands the ancient village of Bainbridge, once the capital of Upper Wensleydale, which was known in the 12th century as the Forest and Manor of Bainbridge. In the background of this picture are the fells of Wensleydale, which still shelter this lovely village.

BISHOP MONKTON, THE VILLAGE THE STREAM AND THE POST OFFICE c1960 B339007

The small stone bridges still cross the beck in front of the village Post Office in the pretty village of Bishop Monkton, south of Ripon in the valley of the River Nidd. It gets its name from a long association with the former monastic community of the nearby city of Ripon.

BOLTON ABBEY C1965 B135064

The great ruined chancel of Bolton Abbey in Wharfedale is one of the great architectural treasures of the Yorkshire Dales. More correctly known as Bolton Priory, the Augustinian house was founded in 1155 and flourished until it was dissolved by Henry VIII in 1539. The nave of the priory was retained; it still serves as the parish church for the Duke of Devonshire's estate village.

BRIMHAM ROCKS C1955 B210020

Cars and buses are no longer allowed to park among the weird and wonderful gritstone formations of Brimham Rocks, near Pateley Bridge in Nidderdale, as they were when this photograph was taken. The 387-acre estate is now in the hands of the National Trust, and visitors have to use the large car park at the entrance before they can explore the wind- and frost-eroded stones.

BUCKDEN, THE VILLAGE c1955 B347032
A flock of white-nosed Swaledale sheep are driven down the road from the village green by a shepherd and his dog in the Upper Wharfedale village of Buckden in the Yorkshire Dales. Buckden is beautifully situated under Buckden Pike, which soars to 2,302 feet above the village and provides a fine viewpoint.

BURLEY-IN-WHARFEDALE, THE PATH TO THE MOORS c1955 B348004
A farmer driving his 'little grey Fergie' tractor turns the hay in this Wharfedale meadow above the village of Burley on a summer's day. The stile in the foreground leads invitingly towards the good walking country which is to be found on the open moor beyond the meadow.

BURNSALL, THE STREET c1955 B252002
Burnsall lies in the heart of Wharfedale, where the drystone walls spread like a net over the fells, as can be seen in the background of this picture. At the end of the Main Street is the spire of St Wilfred's parish church, originally a Saxon foundation, which was 'beautified' in 1612.

BURNSALL, THE RED LION HOTEL c1955 B252012
The ivy-clad Red Lion Hotel is the main hostelry in Burnsall, standing adjacent to the village green in the heart of the village. Note the neat, gritstone cottages with their slabbed, gritstone roofs.

CARPERBY, THE WHEATSHEAF HOTEL c1955 C36001

This view shows the solid Georgian façade of the Wheatsheaf Hotel in the Wensleydale village of Carperby, halfway between Hawes and Leyburn. The inn is typical of many in the villages of the Yorkshire Dales, originally relying on trade from local residents and farmers, but now mainly on tourist traffic.

CARPERBY, THE VILLAGE AND THE CROSS c1955 C36002

Carperby had held a market around its tapered, seven-stepped Market Cross from the 14th century, but it fell into disuse when Askrigg market took over in 1587. But Carperby's market was revived in the 17th century, and the present Market Cross, erected in 1674, dates from that time.

CATTERICK, THE BAY HORSE INN c1965 C50109

There are three village greens in Catterick, the village on the old A1 Great North Road which most people associate with the nearby army garrison. This photograph shows part of the Low Green, with its war memorial and the Bay Horse Inn in the background, and the tower of the parish church of St Anne beyond.

CAWOOD, THE BRIDGE c1955 C258012

Cawood, on the Yorkshire Ouse close to its confluence with the Wharfe, was formerly an important inland port. The ferry across the Ouse played an important part in village life until the bridge in the foreground was built at the end of the 19th century.

CONISTONE, THE VILLAGE c1960 C725008

The limestone village of Conistone in Wharfedale is more correctly known as Conistone-with-Kilnsey, with its twin hamlet sheltering under the impressive overhang of Kilnsey Crag across the river. Conistone clusters around its maypole on the village green, and is still just as dependent on farming as when this photograph, complete with free-range hens in the right foreground, was taken.

FOUNTAINS ABBEY c1955 F42047

Abbot Huby's magnificent north tower at Fountains Abbey, in the valley of the River Skell near Ripon, is a Yorkshire landmark virtually unchanged since the 12th century when it was built. The former Cistercian monastery, with its great east window prominent on the left, still fills the grounds of Studley Royal, but is now served by an award-winning National Trust visitor centre on the hillside above.

GAYLES, THE BAY HORSE INN c1960 G330006

The stone-mullioned windows and sturdy, stone-built construction mark the Bay Horse Inn in the tiny North Yorkshire village of Gayles, north of Richmond, as a building of some antiquity. The lean-to extension on the right served as the village shop when this photograph was taken.

GRASSINGTON, THE SQUARE c1960 G46073

Parked cars fill the cobbled square at Grassington, the pretty Wharfedale village whose wealth was founded on lead mining in the nearby limestone hills. Grassington is still one of the most popular among Dales villages for the tourist, and scenes of congestion like this one are still common today.

HARROGATE, CAMBRIDGE CRESCENT c1955 H26118

'The Prisoner of Zenda' was showing at the Regal Cinema in the elegant North Yorkshire spa town of Harrogate when this picture was taken. The view looking down Cambridge Crescent, busy with shoppers, shows the corner of the parish church of St Peter on the extreme right, in front of the cinema.

HORTON-IN-RIBBLESDALE, THE VILLAGE c1960 H216005

Here we see a quiet corner of the Ribblesdale village of Horton-in-Ribblesdale. Horton is a Mecca for walkers attempting the arduous one-day marathon known as the Yorkshire Three Peaks, and O Short, whose café can be seen on the right, undoubtedly provided pots of tea for them as well as for the cyclists whom he showed on his sign.

ILKLEY, BROOK STREET c1965 I6081

Although technically part of West Yorkshire, the market town of Ilkley, standing at the entrance to Wharfedale, is best-known as the gateway to the Dales. With a history stretching back to the Romans, and a short period as a 19th-century spa, Ilkley's situation on the edge of the famous Ilkley Moor was always its greatest asset. This view shows Brook Street with its cantilever railway bridge, removed after the line closed between Ilkley and Morecambe.

LEYBURN, THE MARKET PLACE c1960 L42023

The Army, probably from the neighbouring garrison town of Catterick, was on parade in the sloping, rectangular Market Place at Leyburn in Wensleydale when the Frith photographer called for this picture. There was not much of an audience to watch the troops as they marched past the Black Swan Hotel in the centre of the picture, although there were a few curious bystanders.

LOW ROW, THE PUNCH BOWL INN c1960 L169007

Cattle graze the green outside the Punch Bowl Inn at Low Row in Swaledale. Low Row is one of several pretty villages which mark the length of Swaledale, many people's favourite among the Yorkshire Dales, with its spectacular scenery and long history of lead mining.

LOW ROW, THE POST OFFICE AND THE CHURCH c1955 L169019

Another view of Low Row, showing the Post Office and the Methodist Chapel on the right. Methodism was a great uniting force among the communities of lead miners in places like Swaledale, and almost every village had its chapel.

MALHAM, THE VILLAGE c1955 M139007

Malham is one of the great showplaces of the Yorkshire Dales, with its scenic splendours of Malham Cove and Gordale Scar, carved in limestone. The Buck Hotel, seen in the centre of the picture, is still a popular hostelry, while the Airedale Hotel on the left provided lunches and teas for the fast-expanding tourist market, in addition to accommodation.

MIDDLEHAM, MARKET PLACE c1955 M70075

The weathered steps of the ancient Market Cross at Middleham show the antiquity of this medieval township at the mouth of Wensleydale. It is now famous for its race horses and historic castle, once the home of Richard, Duke of York and later King Richard III. The elegant, mainly Georgian houses which surround the square include the Black Bull and White Swan Inns.

MUKER, FROM RIGG ROAD c1955 M150006

This is a classic view of the picturesque former lead mining village of Muker in Swaledale, taken from over the Straw Beck from the Rigg Road. This scene has hardly changed today, although the unsightly telegraph pole has been removed.

REETH, THE GREEN c1960 R238048

Here we see the extensive village green at Reeth, the largest village in Swaledale. Cars and buses are parked haphazardly on the green, which is surrounded by public houses such as the Black Bull (centre) and the King's Arms (right). In the background is the long profile and cliffs of Fremlington Edge, where chert was once mined.

REETH, THE VILLAGE c1960 R238050
Another view of Reeth, looking down across the gritstone-slabbed roofs of the cottages of the village, which was another important lead mining centre during the 18th and 19th centuries. In the foreground, three villagers pass the time of day as they cross a sloping green.

RICHMOND, THE MARKET PLACE c1965 R32071
Richmond, the capital of Swaledale, has been described as one of the most perfect market towns in England. This view shows its sloping, circular, cobbled Market Place, with the tower of Holy Trinity Church, now a museum for the Green Howards Regiment from nearby Catterick Garrison, on the right.

SKIPTON, HIGH STREET c1955 S137035

The wide High Street of the town of Skipton on the River Aire was the scene of a weekly livestock market until well into the 20th century, but it now accommodates a general street market on Mondays, Wednesdays and Fridays. At the end of the street is the tower of the parish church of Holy Trinity, which was originally built at the same time as Skipton's 12th-century castle.

WENSLEY, THE VILLAGE c1960 W52008

A workman (centre) scythes the grass on the village green at Wensley. Wensley was the major settlement in the dale of the River Ure which takes its name until 1563, when the plague struck and the village was deserted. Leyburn then took over from Wensley as the capital of the dale, and Wensley never regained its former importance.

Index

The Francis Frith Collection Titles

www.francisfrith.co.uk

The Francis Frith Collection publishes over 100 new titles each year. A selection of those currently available is listed below. For latest catalogue please contact The Francis Frith Collection. **Town Books** 96 pages, approximately 75 photos. **County and Themed Books** 128 pages, approximately 135 photos (unless specified). All titles hardback with laminated case and jacket, except those indicated pb (paperback)

Accrington Old and New
Alderley Edge and Wilmslow
Amersham, Chesham and Rickmansworth
Andover
Around Abergavenny
Around Alton
Aylesbury
Barnstaple
Bedford
Bedfordshire
Berkshire Living Memories
Berkshire PA
Blackpool Pocket Album
Bognor Regis
Bournemouth
Bradford
Bridgend
Bridport
Brighton and Hove
Bristol
Buckinghamshire
Calne Living Memories
Camberley PA
Canterbury Cathedral
Cardiff Old and New
Chatham and the Medway Towns
Chelmsford
Chepstow Then and Now
Cheshire
Cheshire Living Memories
Chester
Chesterfield
Chigwell
Christchurch
Churches of East Cornwall
Clevedon
Clitheroe
Corby Living Memories
Cornish Coast
Cornwall Living Memories
Cotswold Living Memories
Cotswold Pocket Album
Coulsdon, Chipstead and Woodmanstern
County Durham
Cromer, Sheringham and Holt
Dartmoor Pocket Album
Derby
Derbyshire
Derbyshire Living Memories
Devon
Devon Churches
Dorchester

Dorset Coast PA
Dorset Living Memories
Dorset Villages
Down the Dart
Down the Severn
Down the Thames
Dunmow, Thaxted and Finchingfield
Durham
East Anglia PA
East Devon
East Grinstead
Edinburgh
Ely and The Fens
Essex PA
Essex Second Selection
Essex: The London Boroughs
Exeter
Exmoor
Falmouth
Farnborough, Fleet and Aldershot
Folkestone
Frome
Furness and Cartmel Peninsulas
Glamorgan
Glasgow
Glastonbury
Gloucester
Gloucestershire
Greater Manchester
Guildford
Hailsham
Hampshire
Harrogate
Hastings and Bexhill
Haywards Heath Living Memories
Heads of the Valleys
Heart of Lancashire PA
Helston
Herefordshire
Horsham
Humberside PA
Huntingdon, St Neots and St Ives
Hythe, Romney Marsh and Ashford
Ilfracombe
Ipswich PA
Isle of Wight
Isle of Wight Living Memories
King's Lynn
Kingston upon Thames
Lake District PA
Lancashire Living Memories
Lancashire Villages

Available from your local bookshop or from the publisher

The Francis Frith Collection Titles (continued)

Lancaster, Morecombe and Heysham Pocket Album
Leeds PA
Leicester
Leicestershire
Lincolnshire Living Memoires
Lincolnshire Pocket Album
Liverpool and Merseyside
London PA
Ludlow
Maidenhead
Maidstone
Malmesbury
Manchester PA
Marlborough
Matlock
Merseyside Living Memories
Nantwich and Crewe
New Forest
Newbury Living Memories
Newquay to St Ives
North Devon Living Memories
North London
North Wales
North Yorkshire
Northamptonshire
Northumberland
Northwich
Nottingham
Nottinghamshire PA
Oakham
Odiham Then and Now
Oxford Pocket Album
Oxfordshire
Padstow
Pembrokeshire
Penzance
Petersfield Then and Now
Plymouth
Poole and Sandbanks
Preston PA
Ramsgate Old and New
Reading Pocket Album
Redditch Living Memories
Redhill to Reigate
Rhondda Valley Living Mems
Richmond
Ringwood
Rochdale
Romford PA
Salisbury PA
Scotland
Scottish Castles
Sevenoaks and Tonbridge
Sheffield and South Yorkshire PA
Shropshire
Somerset
South Devon Coast
South Devon Living Memories
South East London
Southampton PA
Southend PA

Southport
Southwold to Aldeburgh
Stourbridge Living Memories
Stratford upon Avon
Stroud
Suffolk
Suffolk PA
Surrey Living Memories
Sussex
Sutton
Swanage and Purbeck
Swansea Pocket Album
Swindon Living Memories
Taunton
Teignmouth
Tenby and Saundersfoot
Tiverton
Torbay
Truro
Uppingham
Villages of Kent
Villages of Surrey
Villages of Sussex PA
Wakefield and the Five Towns Living Memories
Warrington
Warwick
Warwickshire PA
Wellingborough Living Memories
Wells
Welsh Castles
West Midlands PA
West Wiltshire Towns
West Yorkshire
Weston-super-Mare
Weymouth
Widnes and Runcorn
Wiltshire Churches
Wiltshire Living memories
Wiltshire PA
Wimborne
Winchester PA
Windermere
Windsor
Wirral
Wokingham and Bracknell
Woodbridge
Worcester
Worcestershire
Worcestershire Living Memories
Wyre Forest
York PA
Yorkshire
Yorkshire Coastal Memories
Yorkshire Dales
Yorkshire Revisited

See Frith books on the internet at www.francisfrith.co.uk

FRITH PRODUCTS & SERVICES

Francis Frith would doubtless be pleased to know that the pioneering publishing venture he started in 1860 still continues today. Over a hundred and forty years later, The Francis Frith Collection continues in the same innovative tradition and is now one of the foremost publishers of vintage photographs in the world. Some of the current activities include:

Interior Decoration

Today Frith's photographs can be seen framed and as giant wall murals in thousands of pubs, restaurants, hotels, banks, retail stores and other public buildings throughout the country. In every case they enhance the unique local atmosphere of the places they depict and provide reminders of gentler days in an increasingly busy and frenetic world.

Product Promotions

Frith products are used by many major companies to promote the sales of their own products or to reinforce their own history and heritage. Frith promotions have been used by Hovis bread, Courage beers, Scots Porage Oats, Colman's mustard, Cadbury's foods, Mellow Birds coffee, Dunhill pipe tobacco, Guinness, and Bulmer's Cider.

Genealogy and Family History

As the interest in family history and roots grows world-wide, more and more people are turning to Frith's photographs of Great Britain for images of the towns, villages and streets where their ancestors lived; and, of course, photographs of the churches and chapels where their ancestors were christened, married and buried are an essential part of every genealogy tree and family album.

Frith Products

All Frith photographs are available Framed or just as Mounted Prints and Posters (size 23 x 16 inches). These may be ordered from the address below. From time to time other products - Address Books, Calendars, Table Mats, etc - are available.

The Internet

Already ninety thousand Frith photographs can be viewed and purchased on the internet through the Frith websites and a myriad of partner sites.

For more detailed information on Frith companies and products, look at these sites:

www.francisfrith.co.uk
www.francisfrith.com
(for North American visitors)

See the complete list of Frith Books at:

www.francisfrith.co.uk

This web site is regularly updated with the latest list of publications from The Francis Frith Collection. If you wish to buy books relating to another part of the country that your local bookshop does not stock, you may purchase on-line.

For further information, trade, or author enquiries please contact us at the address below:
The Francis Frith Collection, Frith's Barn, Teffont, Salisbury, Wiltshire, England SP3 5QP.
Tel: +44 (0)1722 716 376 Fax: +44 (0)1722 716 881 Email: sales@francisfrith.co.uk

See Frith books on the internet at www.francisfrith.co.uk

FREE PRINT OF YOUR CHOICE

Mounted Print
Overall size 14 x 11 inches (355 x 280mm)

Choose any Frith photograph in this book.
Simply complete the Voucher opposite and return it with your remittance for £2.25 (to cover postage and handling) and we will print the photograph of your choice in SEPIA (size 11 x 8 inches) and supply it in a cream mount with a burgundy rule line (overall size 14 x 11 inches).
Please note: photographs with a reference number starting with a "Z" are not Frith photographs and cannot be supplied under this offer.
Offer valid for delivery to one UK address only.

PLUS: Order additional Mounted Prints at HALF PRICE - £7.49 each (normally £14.99)
If you would like to order more Frith prints from this book, possibly as gifts for friends and family, you can buy them at half price (with no additional postage and handling costs).

PLUS: Have your Mounted Prints framed
For an extra £14.95 per print you can have your mounted print(s) framed in an elegant polished wood and gilt moulding, overall size 16 x 13 inches (no additional postage and handling required).

IMPORTANT!

These special prices are only available if you use this form to order . You must use the ORIGINAL VOUCHER on this page (no copies permitted). We can only despatch to one UK address. This offer cannot be combined with any other offer.

Send completed Voucher form to:
The Francis Frith Collection, Frith's Barn, Teffont, Salisbury, Wiltshire SP3 5QP

CHOOSE A PHOTOGRAPH FROM THIS BOOK

Voucher for **FREE** and Reduced Price Frith Prints

Please do not photocopy this voucher. Only the original is valid, so please fill it in, cut it out and return it to us with your order.

Picture ref no	Page no	Qty	Mounted @ £7.49	Framed + £14.95	Total Cost £
		1	Free of charge*	£	£
			£7.49	£	£
			£7.49	£	£
			£7.49	£	£
			£7.49	£	£
			£7.49	£	£

Please allow 28 days for delivery.
Offer available to one UK address only

* Post & handling	£2.25
Total Order Cost	£

Title of this book . . . .

I enclose a cheque/postal order for £ . . . .
made payable to 'The Francis Frith Collection'

OR please debit my Mastercard / Visa / Maestro / Amex card, details below

Card Number

Issue No (Maestro only)   Valid from (Maestro)

Expires   Signature

Name Mr/Mrs/Ms . . . .
Address . . . .
. . . .
. . . .
. . . . Postcode . . . .
Daytime Tel No . . . .
Email . . . .

ISBN 1-85937-397-6   Valid to 31/12/07

Free Print – see overleaf

Would you like to find out more about Francis Frith?

We have recently recruited some entertaining speakers who are happy to visit local groups, clubs and societies to give an illustrated talk documenting Frith's travels and photographs. If you are a member of such a group and are interested in hosting a presentation, we would love to hear from you.

Our speakers bring with them a small selection of our local town and county books, together with sample prints. They are happy to take orders. A small proportion of the order value is donated to the group who have hosted the presentation. The talks are therefore an excellent way of fundraising for small groups and societies.

Can you help us with information about any of the Frith photographs in this book?

We are gradually compiling an historical record for each of the photographs in the Frith archive. It is always fascinating to find out the names of the people shown in the pictures, as well as insights into the shops, buildings and other features depicted.

If you recognize anyone in the photographs in this book, or if you have information not already included in the author's caption, do let us know. We would love to hear from you, and will try to publish it in future books or articles.

Our production team

Frith books are produced by a small dedicated team at offices in the converted Grade II listed 18th-century barn at Teffont near Salisbury, illustrated above. Most have worked with the Frith Collection for many years. All have in common one quality: they have a passion for the Frith Collection. The team is constantly expanding, but currently includes:

Paul Baron, Phillip Brennan, Jason Buck, John Buck, Ruth Butler, Heather Crisp, David Davies, Louis du Mont, Isobel Hall, Lucy Hart, Julian Hight, Peter Horne, James Kinnear, Karen Kinnear, Tina Leary, Stuart Login, David Marsh, Sue Molloy, Glenda Morgan, Wayne Morgan, Sarah Roberts, Kate Rotondetto, Dean Scource, Eliza Sackett, Terence Sackett, Sandra Sampson, Adrian Sanders, Sandra Sanger, Julia Skinner, Miles Smith, Lewis Taylor, Shelley Tolcher, Lorraine Tuck, David Turner, Amanita Wainwright and Ricky Williams.